TEACHING BASICS
PRESCHOOL

A TEACHER CERTIFICATION BOOK

By *Mavis Weidman*
and
By *Daryl Dale*

CHRISTIAN EDUCATION OFFICE
The Christian and Missionary Alliance
Nyack, New York

Prepared and typeset by the
Christian Education Office
The Christian and Missionary Alliance
Nyack, New York

Printed by
Christian Publications
3825 Hartzdale Drive
Camp Hill, PA 17011

Order additional copies from
Christian Publications
Publishing House of The Christian and Missionary Alliance
3825 Hartzdale Drive, Camp Hill, PA 17011

Contents

Chapter   *Page*
1   A Divine Appointment   5

2   The Child You Teach   9

3   Preschool Children Do Learn   15

4   Learning through Doing   21

5   The Teaching Team   29

6   The Preschool Classroom   33

7   Planning the Hour   37

8   Learning Centers Are Teaching Centers 41

9   Organizing Learning Centers   49

10   Music with Young Children   55

11   Lesson Preparation   59

12   Parent Teacher Relationships   65

13   Love Makes the Difference   71

     Notes and Bibliography   75

CHAPTER 1
A DIVINE APPOINTMENT

Congratulations! Congratulations on becoming a member of a highly influential group—teachers of young children in Sunday school. As you take your place as a preschool teacher, you are filling a God-ordained position. You are obeying the great commission which is given to every Christian. You are investing your talents for eternal dividends.

Your influence on young children can be so great that it will extend beyond time and into eternity. Enter into your teaching assignment with joy and anticipation. Consider it a God-given opportunity. Use the resources your Sunday school purchases to the best of your ability. Be assured that those resources, combined with your love, will be used by the miracle-working God to permanently affect the emotional patterns and habit structures your young pupils are forming. Your place in God's program is of the utmost importance. Rejoice in your teaching privilege.

AN APPOINTMENT TO DEMONSTRATE GOD'S LOVE

You may be a department superintendent, a teacher or a helper. Whoever you are you have been entrusted to introduce little ones to the things of God. Today, we understand as never before the tremendous importance of the preschool years. The child learns more in his first five years of life than during any other 5-year period. By the age of 5 or 6, a child's emotional pattern and habit structure are formed. During these preschool years, you are laying the foundations for character, attitudes and response to the things of God. During the time the child is in your class he is pliable and eager to respond. You are leading him in his first responses to spiritual truth.

You must earn the right to a special place in the heart and life of these young children. This love and friendship cannot be limited to Sunday morning. It takes contact during the week. It takes time, energy and willingness to give of yourself. Make it your goal to enter the child's world, to become his best adult friend. With this friendship comes the opportunity to be a roll-model in a very special way as you demonstrate God's love.

AN APPOINTMENT TO BUILD A CLASS

As you look at the boys and girls in your department, remember that statistics show three out of five of these children will drop out of Sunday school before they graduate from high school. Determine that your class will have no dropouts. Determine that you will do ANYTHING to prevent the loss of even one pupil on your roll. Every pupil has been given you by God. Take good care of them. Young Samuels or Timothys may now be in your preschool department. If your concern is great enough, you have opportunity to influence not only the young child with his great potential, but also his parents. No effort is too great to expend when you know that attitudes of eternal importance are being established in these formative years.

As you seek to build your class you will continually be looking for ways to reach new children and their families. You will build prospect lists from Cradle Roll contacts and from visitation efforts. You will look for prospects from those who attend church time but fail to come to Sunday school. A good preschool department will have an active outreach program. You have an appointment to build a class!

AN APPOINTMENT TO SHARE THE WORD

The Bible may be just a black book to many of your pupils. It is your responsibility to help them to understand that the Bible is a special book that tells about God and Jesus. Hold the Bible in your hand as you make the Bible stories come alive. Relate the Bible verses to a child's everyday experiences. As the preschooler observes how you handle the Bible and your tone of voice as you talk about it, he is forming important attitudes about the Word of God. Be sure that you know the Bible stories so well that you can tell them with interest and enthusiasm.

Your divine appointment cannot be taken lightly. As you sense your high calling, you will want to fulfill your commitment in the best way possible. Read widely, attend workshops, visit other Sunday schools or nursery schools. Be eager to learn the best possible methods to use with young children. Be flexible enough to try them. God has called you to be faithful in the service opportunity He has granted to you. Be encouraged as you claim the promise from John 15:16, "I have chosen you, and ordained you, that you should go and bring forth fruit, and that your fruit should remain."

QUIZ

1. Every teacher has received

    a) a divine appointment
    b) training
    c) exceptional teaching skills

2. Every teacher should determine that his class shall have

    a) no behavior problems
    b) no dropouts
    c) no unsaved pupils

3. God has called the teacher to

    a) be faithful
    b) change lives
    c) sacrifice everything

4. Teachers of preschoolers should

    a) teach many Bible verses
    b) handle the Bible with reverence
    c) give awards for memory work

5. The preschool child learns

    a) the basics of the Christian faith
    b) less than other children
    c) more than in any other five-year period

CHAPTER 2
THE CHILD YOU TEACH

LITTLE PEOPLE IN SPECIAL CLASSES

There is some confusion in Sunday schools about names for classes of preschoolers. Babies and toddlers are a part of the preschool division. Classes for twos and threes are usually called the Nursery class but this is not to be confused with the baby nursery. Many churches move two-year-olds into the department on their second birthday. All too frequently they are not ready for the program. It is far better to add a toddler story program for children one and two years of age and begin the nursery class when they are 2½. Classes for four- and five-year-olds are called preprimary or kindergarten. For the purpose of this book we will deal with ages 2–5 and call them preschoolers.

A PERSON FULL OF WIGGLES

Preschool children are very active. Their growing bodies are full of wiggles. The wiggles come from their larger muscles. The smaller muscles of the young child are not well-developed, making the use of scissors and detailed coloring difficult. Plan six or eight changes in activity an hour, alternating quiet and active times. Give the children plenty of space. More than for any other age group, preschoolers need room to move.

A PERSON WITH A "LITERAL" MIND

Young children can only think of things they can picture in their minds. It is for this reason that much of their learning comes through their senses of sight, touch, smell and taste. Learning centers are ideal for this sensory learning. They allow frequent child movement and encourage pupils to explore God's world through each of their senses.

The preschooler's ability to learn through hearing is limited by the fact that his mind must be shown before it can comprehend. The young child cannot see "sin," but understands he must obey mother when she says, "Do not touch the cake." The young child does not understand the word "trust," but knows he can pray to Jesus when he is sick.

The preschooler cannot understand symbolism. A heart is a heart. A sheep is a sheep. To "stand" means to put your feet on the floor. The child cannot understand how Jesus, a person, can fit into a little heart or how he, a boy with two legs, is like a sheep with four. "To stand alone on the Word of God" means to put the Bible down on the floor and step on it. The mind of the young child takes everything literally because it thinks in terms of that which he can picture.

The young child's ability to learn through hearing is also limited by his limited vocabulary. Children can only understand words they have heard before. Many adult words are without meaning to a young child. If you want to know how to talk to preschoolers, you will learn best by listening to them. When you use words children don't use, explain their meaning before you use them.

The young child is curious. He is full of questions. Answer and anticipate his questions. Since he says "no" frequently, avoid asking "yes" and "no" questions. The child is discovering he is a separate identity and needs to exert independence. Even though the child's mind is curious, he has difficulty concentrating for more than a few minutes. Generally, every three to five minutes the two-year-old will say, "I've had enough," and get up to walk over to something more interesting. Four- and five-year-olds will concentrate on one activity up to eight minutes.

A PERSON IN A "ME" WORLD

The young child lives in a "me" world, but slowly grows to understand how to live in a "we" world. The two- and three-year-old does his own thing. He knows grown-ups can read him stories, find nice toys and hug real good. Therefore, he likes to be around adults who give him special attention. However, he usually ignores the other children. The young child isn't prepared to live in a "we" world.

The preschool teacher needs to help four- and five-year-olds think of others. She guides the children to think of others by teaching them to sit in a group setting, playing group games and acting out Bible stories. The young child does not have the ability to work on cooperative projects (for example, setting a table together), but can work side by side with other children. The two-year-old knows only a "me" world, but by the time he is five he has learned to live in a "we" world, although he is still very self-centered.

A PERSON EASILY UPSET

Fears are common to the young child. He cannot easily control his emotions. Being unfamiliar or uncertain about a person, classroom or activity is confusing and upsetting. The young child needs familiar surroundings that are quiet, pleasant and comfortable. He needs a loving friend. For this reason it is important to have more than one teacher in a preschool classroom. Never rotate teachers in a preschool department.

The young child's emotions reflect the emotions of the adults in his home and church. The preschool teacher should know the home situation where most emotional problems develop. Be ready to talk about the children's fears and help them to understand that Jesus loves and cares for them. Be the loving friend the young child needs. Let the atmosphere be happy, loving and joyous. Let patience reign.

A PERSON WITH A "LET ME DO IT" ATTITUDE

Young children learn through doing. They enjoy learning new skills as long as the projects are not too difficult or too long. Allow your children to do their own artwork even though it may not look good to you.

A PERSON OF SIMPLE FAITH

The young child is spiritually sensitive. Jesus recognized this sensitivity:

"Let the little children come to me, and do not hinder them, for the kingdom of heaven belongs to such as these" (Matthew 19:14).

"Anyone who will not receive the kingdom of God like a little child will never enter it" (Luke 18:17).

The young child believes everything the teacher says. Teach God's truths carefully, making everything clear. As the children begin to understand and respond to Bible truths (love, trust, obedience), their lives are being prepared to take root and grow in the Word of God. Allow your preschool children to express their joy and praise to God through music. Help them sense God's unchanging love. Give them opportunity to respond to the truth through classroom activities. The preschool teacher is preparing the child so that at the proper time, through the enabling power of the Holy Spirit, he will express faith in Christ and become a born-again child of God's family.

Most preschool children are not ready to receive Christ as Savior. They learn that Jesus loves them and in turn want to love Him. Although the child would respond to a general invitation to "raise your hand," the response most likely would reflect a desire to please the teacher or move around. It probably would not indicate that the child understands the meaning of salvation. Preschool teachers therefore do not give salvation invitations.

When a preschool child is ready to receive Christ as Savior, he will come to you individually. He will ask several questions and you will know of his readiness to receive Christ. The wise teacher will not rush this important decision, but will remember what Paul told Timothy, "And how from infancy you have known the holy scriptures which are able to make you wise unto salvation through faith in Christ Jesus" (II Timothy 3:15). The preschool teacher has an important role in preparing the way for salvation.

The preschool child is a very complex person. Each child matures at his own speed. Know your children. Treat each child as the individual he is. Be familiar with the characteristics that are common to most of them. Teach at their physical, mental and emotional level. Accept their self-centeredness, but lead them to be aware and considerate of others. Remember, you are preparing soil in which the Word of God will take root and grow.

FACTS TO REMEMBER

YOUNG CHILDREN NEED 6–8 CHANGES OF ACTIVITY EVERY HOUR.

THE YOUNG CHILD CANNOT UNDERSTAND SYMBOLISM.

FEARS ARE COMMON TO YOUNG CHILDREN.

THE PRESCHOOL TEACHER PREPARES THE WAY FOR SALVATION.

QUIZ

1. The young child lives in a _____ world.

2. The young child has a _____ attitude.

3. What is the best "medicine" for soothing the emotional preschooler?

   _____

4. How does one learn to talk meaningfully to a preschooler?

   _____

5. List two ways a young child's ability to learn through hearing is limited.

   a. _____

   b. _____

6. Name the two primary ways a teacher will know when a young child is ready to receive Christ.

   a. _____

   b. _____

CHAPTER 3
PRESCHOOL CHILDREN DO LEARN

Preschool children have an incredible ability to learn about God and His Son, Jesus Christ. Although it is important to consider *what* preschoolers can learn, the wise teacher of young children understands that *attitude* aims are more important than *knowledge* aims. Facts are often difficult for the preschool child to remember. He can understand how Jesus gave hungry people food but don't expect him to remember "five loaves and two fish," "5,000 people" and "twelve baskets of food." How a child feels about Jesus is more important than what he knows about Jesus.

WHAT CAN YOUNG CHILDREN LEARN?

STUDY SUBJECT	2- AND 3- YEAR-OLDS	4- AND 5- YEAR-OLDS
GOD What do I want young children to know and feel about **GOD**?	God made me God loves me God cares for my needs God hears me when I talk to Him God made the world and all things in it	God made all people God loves me and I love Him I can talk to God any time and place and He always hears me God is interested in what I do

STUDY SUBJECT	2- AND 3- YEAR-OLDS	4- AND 5- YEAR-OLDS
JESUS What do I want young children to know and feel about **JESUS?**	Jesus is the baby that was born at Christmas Jesus grew like I do Jesus loves me Jesus is my friend. He is always with me Jesus is God's Son Jesus died but today He is alive	God sent Jesus as a baby Jesus is God's Son who lives in heaven Jesus can do hard things no one else can do Jesus loves me and other people too Jesus died on the cross and will forgive my sin if I am sorry
THE BIBLE What do I want young children to know and feel about the **BIBLE?**	The Bible is a special Book The Bible tells us stories about God and Jesus The Bible tells me that Jesus loves me	The Bible is a special Book that tells us about God and Jesus The Bible is God's Word The Bible tells me how to live The Bible is a book of "true" stories
HIMSELF What do I want the young child to know and feel about **HIMSELF?**	I like me! My teacher likes me I'm important to God	I like myself I'm important to God and to my teachers. I make important choices

16

OTHERS What do I want the young child to know and feel about **OTHERS?**	I can be a good helper I can begin to learn to take turns Jesus loves me and others too	God wants me to be kind and help others Other people may not always be kind to me God loves all the children of the world
FAMILY What do I want the young child to know and feel about the **FAMILY?**	I thank God for my family I love my family I can help my mother and father	God gives me a mother and father to take care of me God wants me to obey my parents

All learning charts, especially those for preschoolers, have limitations. The learning abilities of young children vary so much that it is impossible to accurately list learning goals for separate age groups. There is no sudden transition between a three- and a four-year-old. Some three-year-olds will readily respond to four- and five-year-old expectations. Some five-year-olds are not ready to understand that Jesus died for them.

Teachers of preschoolers should look for and expect a response as children begin to discover and understand these truths. As God builds and changes the attitudes of your children, they will naturally want to please Jesus. It is your responsibility to show them how to respond, how to please Jesus. As you prepare your lessons, think through ways in which young children can respond to God in their daily experiences.

Every week he will learn a little more about God, Jesus, the Bible, himself and others. The preschooler will change significantly as he moves from being a dependent baby to a very independent toddler. By the time the preschool child is ready to leave your class and enter the first grade, he will have become a person with a distinct character. You will teach facts, but God changes attitudes. Depend upon God to bring about the attitude and life changes in your children that will serve to draw them to Christ for the rest of their lives.

FACTS TO REMEMBER

PEOPLE TEACH FACTS; GOD CHANGES ATTITUDES.

ATTITUDES LAST FOREVER.

THE PRESCHOOL TEACHER'S CHIEF GOAL IS TO HELP THE CHILD DEVELOP RIGHT SPIRITUAL ATTITUDES.

HOW A CHILD FEELS IS MORE IMPORTANT THAN WHAT HE KNOWS.

QUIZ

1. How a young child _____ about Jesus is more important than what he _____ about Jesus.

2. The teacher's chief goal is to help the child develop right spiritual _____.

3. What can all four-year-olds learn that is beyond the mental capabilities of three-year-olds?

   _____

4. List six general topics which summarize the teaching goals of a preschool teacher:

   a. _____ d. _____

   b. _____ e. _____

   c. _____ f. _____

CHAPTER 4
LEARNING THROUGH DOING

Young children learn through doing. They are continually busy exploring through the senses of touch, sight, hearing, taste, and smell. The more these senses are stimulated the more children tend to remember. The wise teacher selects learning experiences through which the children can use their senses to make discoveries.

THE SENSE OF SIGHT

The sense of sight is continually used in the preschool department. Bible story pictures, drawing, coloring and flannel-graph stories are familiar methods in teaching young children. Consider these creative ways to stimulate a child's sense of sight.

PICTURE SEARCH—Give each child a book or magazine and have them find teaching pictures. FOR EXAMPLE: Children search for "helpers" in the books when the lesson is on helping others. Children find birds or flowers when the lesson is about God providing pretty clothes for birds, flowers and children. The local library provides an excellent source for books.

MAGNIFYING GLASS—At the nature center, provide the children with a large magnifying glass. God's creations are even more wonderful when seen through a magnifying glass.

THE ART TABLE—An art table provides many sensory experiences. Painting activities such as the mixing of colors provides opportunities to talk about how glad we are that God gave us eyes to see pretty colors. Making a collage of various nature materials: twigs, leaves, seashells, cotton balls, etc., allows great imaginative work for fours and fives.

THE SENSE OF HEARING

The child hears the teacher talk and learns through his sense of hearing. Consider these ways to teach your children through their sense of hearing:

CASSETTE RECORDER—Record a story or song and play it for the children. Ask the children questions and record their answers on cassette tape. Bring in sounds found in the story (for example, a storm, baby crying, birds singing, etc.) to supplement your talk. Record the children singing or playing their rhythm-band instruments.

SPECIAL MUSIC—Invite a special guest to play a musical instrument for the children. Have them sing with the guitar, or hum with kazoos.

RECORDS—Play a record or cassette for background music to introduce a new song that teaches the thought for the day.

LISTENING CENTER—The experience of listening can be enhanced by having the child close his eyes and listen to sounds. Sounds may be loud or soft. Wind chimes and alarm clocks are interesting to young children. Containers with rice or beans can be used to teach loud and soft sounds. You can add to these sensory experiences an art table project of having the children make a scrapbook of sounds using magazine pictures. The children should rejoice, "We are glad God gave us ears!"

THE SENSE OF TOUCH

The sense of touch can provide lots of Sunday school fun and reinforce Bible truths.

TOUCH AND FEEL BOX—Have children reach in a box and touch objects they cannot see. It is fun to guess what is in the box. Children may respond, "We are glad God gave us hands to feel things."

NATURE CENTER—Many items used in the nature center are fun to explore through the child's sense of touch. Animals, flowers, shells, rocks, water, ice and other items provide teaching opportunities.

DRESS UP—Putting on a Bible costume is enjoyable to children. The robe, belt, and head scarf help the child to remember Joseph and his pretty clothes or John the Baptist and his coat of fur.

FINGER PAINTING—This is a delightful sensory experience. Children (protected with smocks) love to smear and squish the paint. Shelf paper, liquid starch and a small amount of powdered tempera paint are the materials needed for finger painting. Print a Bible verse on each child's picture to assist the parents in understanding the purpose behind their child's creation.

PLAY DOUGH—Clay is often too hard for children to work with, but play dough is pliable. Children love to squeeze and roll the dough. It allows for creativity or can be used to make objects found within the Bible story.

WATER PLAY—Water play is particularly helpful when the story features water. Use smocks for children as they experiment with things that float and things that sink. Allow the children to blow a small boat across the water, bathe a baby doll or water a plant.

THE SENSE OF SMELL

The sense of smell can be used to reinforce the Sunday school lesson. Think about each story and look for objects or situations that may have had a scent. Can you think of a Bible story in which these smells occurred?

Smoke and fire   Perfume
Flowers   Fish
Freshly baked bread   Baby odors
Fruit   Incense

Not every lesson will provide a teaching opportunity which allows the children to experience the lesson through their noses. Whenever possible, find a way that allows children to use their sense of smell.

THE SENSE OF TASTE

Food is often mentioned in the Bible. Consider these opportunities for using the sense of taste within a lesson plan:

Feeding the five thousand —bread and fish
Manna from heaven   —Cherrios
Fishing from boat   —sardines
Ruth and Boaz   —wheat and grain
                            products
Widow's oil   —olives

For example, for the story of Ruth and Boaz bring wholewheat berries, bran and flour. Let the children taste wheat products—cereal or crackers. Better still all can share in making some muffins to bake in the church kitchen to have for snack time. Or bring an ear of corn, cornmeal or Corn Chex to taste and make corn muffins for snack.

The sense of taste can also be used by having the children make cookies in shapes that will reinforce the lesson. With cookie dough, rolling pins, and the right cookie cutters children can make sheep, flowers, angels or other objects found in the Bible story. If the cookies are made early in the Sunday school hour, they may be baked in the church kitchen and eaten at the end of the hour.

The sense of taste can also be easily utilized when studying about a missionary or child in a foreign country. Bring foods from that country for children to taste.

It is important to plan time for children to taste flavors and foods during the lesson hour. Learning through the sense of taste should not be limited to snack time.

A SAMPLE SENSORY LESSON

While studying creation, read to the children the book *How God Gave Us Peanut Butter* by Mary LeBar. Bring peanuts in the shell for children to observe and taste. Have children place shelled peanuts in a blender. Children will be delighted as you make your own peanut butter. Take the lid off occasionally to let children smell the delightful aroma. With careful supervision they can all have a part of putting the peanuts in the blender. They hear the noise of the blender at work. If there is time, they can help make the sandwiches to enjoy at snack time. This project provides a perfect morning of sensory experience. "How glad we are that God gave us eyes to see, noses to smell, tongues to taste, and hands to help."

Teach young children through their five senses. In planning your lesson and setting up learning centers each week, try to utilize as many of the child's senses as possible. Evaluate your lesson plan by asking yourself these five questions.

- Will the children hear this lesson in a special way?
- How will the children explore today's truth through their sense of touch?
- Is there a special smell in today's lesson that I could bring to class?

- Does the story include food, grain or drink that children could taste?
- Have I prepared a lesson that will touch four of the child's five senses?

TEACHING THROUGH PRACTICING

Children learn through doing. Young children learn through repetition. Practice is repeatedly doing the same thing over and over again until it is learned. Preschoolers need to be given opportunities to practice good habits every Sunday. Practice is often done in the home center but can be planned for almost any area of the room.

Young children need to learn to thank God for their food. Saying grace is a Christian habit that needs to be practiced. When the lesson for the day is on "Thanking God for Our Food," the teacher should plan many practice times for children to thank God for their food.

EXAMPLE: Children find pictures of good food in magazines. The pictures are pasted to paper plates and prayer is said before the children pretend to eat. Children sit around the table and say "Thank You, God" before eating oyster crackers. Later children are given a carrot or celery stick. Just before the teacher hands them out, children thank God. Juice is brought to class and children thank God again before drinking juice. Each time of thanks is said with bowed heads and folded hands.

Notice how many times the children practiced thanking God for food before they ate. The more children practice a behavior the more likely they are to go home and live that behavior. Children learn habits of prayer, helping, cleaning-up, kindness, thanks, obedience, etc., through repeated practice. Whenever a Bible lesson teaches Christian behavior plan to incorporate practice methods.

Practice usually involves several of the child's five senses. Children learn through doing.

FACTS TO REMEMBER

PLAN PRESCHOOL PRACTICE ACTIVITIES.

ALLOW YOUNG CHILDREN TO TASTE AND SMELL THE LESSON.

CONSIDER YOUR TEACHING ASSIGNMENT A DI-VINE APPOINTMENT.

LOVE IS EVIDENCED ON TUESDAY AS WELL AS SUNDAY.

EARLY FORMATIVE YEARS ARE OF ETERNAL IMPORTANCE.

QUIZ

1. An excellent source for books on a preschool level is the

   _____.

2. A child's sense of _____ is
   probably the most difficult to utilize in teaching lessons.

3. The preschool teacher should attempt to touch _____

   _____ of the child's five senses in every lesson.

4. In order to develop good habits, lesson time needs to be

   given to _____ desired
   behaviors.

5. List five special methods listed in this chapter that focus
   on the child's sense of hearing.

   a. _____

   b. _____

   c. _____

   d. _____

   e. _____

6. List two general ways the teacher can utilize a child's
   sense of taste in teaching a Bible story.

   a. _____

   b. _____

CHAPTER 5
THE TEACHING TEAM

It has been well said that if we are to make God real to a young child, we must surround him with teachers to whom God is real. The worker with young children must be happy, understanding, flexible and imaginative. The staff should include men and women. Children need to associate men with Christian truths and the "father image" is important.

The maximum number of children for a room of two- and three-year-olds is 15 and for four- and five-year-olds is 20. The ratio of workers to children should be 1 to 4 for twos and threes and 1 to 5 for fours and fives. There should always be two people in the room no matter how small the class. The low ratio is important since the best teaching of preschoolers is in the small group and in one-to-one relationships. One of the persons should be designated the DEPARTMENT SUPERINTENDENT. This is an important organizational step because one person needs to be responsible for planning and coordinating the program for the hour.

The department superintendent is not a leader of opening exercises, but an organizing leader. There are no classes, but TEACHERS work together as a team throughout the hour. The department superintendent prepares the lesson plan, collects teaching materials, sets up the classroom and learning centers. An example of a "Lesson Planning Sheet" is on page 30. Notice how the theme, aim, Bible verse, songs and conversation thoughts all focus on one topic. The superintendent gives a copy of this lesson plan to each person on the staff. Each teacher can clearly see her learning center responsibilities and the materials needed for each activity.

LESSON PLANNING SHEET

Unit Theme: We want to be Jesus helpers   Date: May 12

Lesson Theme: Dorcas is a kind neighbor

Lesson Aim: To be God's helper at home ... by putting silverware on the table

Bible Verse: Trust in the Lord and do good   Scripture: Acts 9: 36-42

Songs and Finger Play to use throughout the hour: "God can help" –
"I can help" – Helping Action Rhyme ... p. 55

Conversation Thoughts: Suggestions for helping at home

*= together times

LEARNING CENTERS	PERSON RESPONSIBLE	MATERIALS NEEDED
#1 Art Center • make placemats (table setting and decorate placemat)	Lucy	for each child: • 12x18 construction paper • dinner size paper plates • crayons
#2 Home Living Center • practice setting the table, etc.	Jim	• tablecloth • sufficient plates and cutlery to set the table
#3 * Story Circle	Mary	• puppet from teaching aid packet • Dorcas Bible picture • household items & clothing to illustrate Dorcas story
#4 * Playing the Story	Mary	
#5 Bulletin Board Center	Jim	• helping hands to put on the bulletin board • teaching aid packet
#6 Art Center making a helping game	Lucy	• following handwork instructions Project 11
#7 Music Center * Conversation about things mother does	Mary	• cassette player • Cassette #1 – motions in music "Mother's Hands"
#8 Art Center * Workbooks	Jim	• crayons • paste • My Bible TiME Book direction p. 23
#9		

As the children arrive, they will choose either the ART CENTER or the HOME LIVING CENTER. The department superintendent has all materials laid out. All the children will be encouraged to make the placemats. Then they will gather in the STORY CIRCLE for the Bible story and then enjoy PLAYING the story of Dorcas the helper. During this time Jim and Lucy are getting the materials ready for the BULLETIN BOARD activity and the helping GAME at the ART CENTER. Children move between these centers. Music calls them for a TOGETHER TIME at the music center with Mary during which time Jim gets the pupil activity books and needed materials laid out on the tables.

The departmental superintendent will find it helpful to gather all the teachers for a monthly planning meeting. Teachers can study the unit theme, share creative teaching ideas, plan learning centers, evaluate previous lessons and begin to plan for the new unit. The planning meeting builds a strong teaching team.

The preschool department should designate one person as the SECRETARY. Young children don't know addresses, phone numbers or birthdays. However, it is very important to search out this data and plan to follow-up visitors and absentees.

Ideally the preschool division should have a director who coordinates and develops the total program for young children. The division includes Cradle Roll, Babies, Toddlers, twos and threes and fours and fives.

FACTS TO REMEMBER

INCLUDE MEN ON THE TEACHING TEAM.

LESS THAN TWO IS TOO FEW.

THE DEPARTMENT SUPERINTENDENT PLANS AND COORDINATES THE ACTIVITIES FOR THE HOUR.

QUIZ

1. The preschool department superintendent does not lead

   _____.

2. A teacher-pupil ratio of _____ is needed for twos and threes.

3. In the preschool department there are no classes.

   Therefore, teachers work together as a _____ throughout the teaching hour.

4. The department superintendent gives each teacher a copy

   of the _____ before Sunday.

5. Why is it difficult to be a secretary in a preschool department? _____

6. What does it mean, "Less than two is too few"?

   _____

7. List three responsibilities of the department superintendent.

   a. _____

   b. _____

   c. _____

8. What two pieces of information are listed beside each learning center activity on the "Lesson Planning Sheet"?

   a. _____

   b. _____

CHAPTER 6
THE PRESCHOOL CLASSROOM

A pastor with a Sunday school of over 1,000, when asked what he would do to build up a Sunday school if it were small, replied that he would promote a large Cradle Roll and Nursery department with a corresponding emphasis on young adults. Continuing his thought he said, "These are the two most vital areas in an expanding program."

Even the small Sunday school with ten preschoolers should plan for a minimum of three rooms for this division: A baby nursery for babies and toddlers, a department for twos and threes and a department for fours and fives. Large schools will divide the twos and threes and the fours and fives.

ROOMS

Preschoolers need more floor space than any other group in Sunday school. The rooms should be on the ground floor allowing approximately 25–30 square feet per child. Carpeting or a story rug is always desired. Windows should be low enough so children can see out. Rest room facilities should be nearby. Rectangular rooms provide maximum flexibility. However, the size of the room is more important than shape. Never put young children in a multipurpose room with folding partitions.

Even a room with minimal equipment can provide *four* basic teaching areas. All of the teaching must not take place around a table in the middle of the room. The *tables* are usually used for a nature center and for art and handwork activities. The children can work at the *walls* in decorating a bulletin board or pasting pictures to a mural. The *floor* can be used for building with blocks, acting out stories, looking at books and playing games. The *chairs* can be used not only for listening or singing but also for group activities. For example, arrange chairs like a bus or train and sing "Here we go riding, riding to church on Sunday."

EQUIPMENT

Chairs should be 10–14″ from the floor and the table tops 10″ higher than the chairs. No adult-size chairs are needed as the teachers should work at the child's eye level. Small *tables* are preferable (tops 30″ x 48″ with washable surface). Never use huge kidney-shaped tables that confine the children around the teacher. Pianos are not needed. A couple of *bulletin boards* are desirable. They should be set 12″ from the floor. Pictures should always be placed at eye level. If you do not have a carpeted room, try to have a *story rug.* This makes it unnecessary to move chairs at story time. When you use an easel, place it at the child's eye level. Remain seated while telling the story. You will need *low shelves* where the children can help themselves to supplies. *Cabinets* for the teacher's supplies mounted on the wall will save floor space. As soon as possible, include the *learning center equipment* described in Chapter 9.

Attendance can often be encouraged or hindered by the facilities provided. If the rooms are crowded and unattractive, the children become restless, have a tendency to cry and may not want to return. If you have to work in undesirable rooms, choose room for movement over large tables. When a building program is under way, make sure you plan well for preschoolers!

FACTS TO REMEMBER

PRESCHOOL CHILDREN NEED SPACE.

EVERY ROOM HAS A MINIMUM OF FOUR TEACHING AREAS.

EYE LEVEL IS THE ONLY LEVEL FOR THE YOUNG CHILD.

QUIZ

1. What are the three preschool divisions recommended for a small Sunday school with ten young children?

   _____

2. How high should the bottom of a bulletin board be set on the wall of a preschool classroom?

   _____

3. What is the most important quality in a preschool classroom?

   _____

4. List four teaching areas found within almost all classrooms.

   a. _____ c. _____

   b. _____ d. _____

5. List four things in the preschool classroom that should be at a child's eye level.

   a. _____ c. _____

   b. _____ d. _____

6. The teacher should _____ _____ while telling the story.

CHAPTER 7
PLANNING THE HOUR

In "Total Hour Teaching" everything during the hour points toward the one central theme or Bible truth.

As an adult observed a preschool department engaged in a variety of informal activities the question was asked, "Don't you teach them anything?" "No," the department superintendent answered, "but we HELP THEM LEARN a great deal." This is the key. Children are learning from the minute they walk into the room. They learn by smelling, tasting, touching, seeing and hearing. Everything that happens in the room is designed to HELP THEM LEARN.

ARRIVAL TIME

This period includes presession and continues for up to one-half hour. Arrival begins at the time a pupil enters the classroom, not 9:45 A.M. The teacher welcomes the pupil by name and compliments the pupil on something. Once welcomed, the children are free to engage in their choice of a number of learning center activities. A teacher or helper should be at each teaching center to use the activity as a springboard to conversation about the Bible truth of the day. This is an individualized approach to learning. With a little gentle direction the children can be involved in all of the centers that are important to the theme of the day.

An important principle to guide you in preparing your lesson activities is called "change of pace." Your lesson plan (see page 30) will include six or more activities, alternating quiet and active times so the children don't get restless. You can estimate how much time you will need for each activity, but many times you will have to be guided by the response of the children. If they are ready to move on, be flexible. It is for this reason we do not provide a chart to indicate how to divide the hour. You may not always be able to do everything you have planned, but you will be consciously working toward your teaching aims for the entire hour.

TOGETHER TIMES

Together times will usually come at different times during the hour. A signal, such as a bell, will call the children from the learning centers to the story circle. Always remember that the Bible story is the most important part of the hour and plan accordingly. There may be music before or after the story or at different times during the hour. Lead the children in prayer in short, simple words and sentences. The words should express the children's prayer. If you are going to play the story, the children will probably all participate. If a child holds back, let him watch until he is ready.

HANDWORK AND ACTIVITY-BOOK TIME

Handwork may take place at a table, the bulletin board or the "Art Center." Several handwork activities may be included in

the lesson. There is usually a handwork activity at the end of the hour to reinforce the theme of the Bible story and to help the child see how the teaching fits into his own life. This closing handwork activity is the part of the curriculum which makes it possible for the child to carry the Bible truth home in concrete form to share with his family. It also serves as a reminder of the lesson. Your teacher's book will usually suggest conversation ideas to add meaning to the work the children are doing. Have all handwork materials ready before time to start. Make a sample of each project to show children how theirs will look.

For very young children the handwork serves as a "Story Reminder" which the teacher prepares. It is used at the end of the story as a personalized review and then as a reminder to parents of the lesson for the day. "Story Reminders" are well worth the preparation time. Usually ladies from an adult class can be recruited to help with the preparation.

The arrival, together and handwork times are the framework of every preschool Sunday school hour. However, never forget to utilize learning centers and plan a minimum of six to eight activities for every teaching hour.

FACTS TO REMEMBER

ALL ACTIVITIES IN THE HOUR POINT TOWARD A CENTRAL THEME.

CHANGE OF PACE IS THE KEY TO PLANNING.

THE BIBLE TRUTH IS REINFORCED WITH "TAKE HOME" HANDWORK.

QUIZ

TRUE OR FALSE

1. ____ Handwork provided by the curriculum takes too much time to prepare.

2. ____ It is important for all the children to participate in playing the story.

3. ____ It is important to use all of the material suggested in the teacher's manual.

4. ____ The teacher should reserve 15 minutes for telling the story.

5. ____ Start the Sunday school class promptly at 9:45 A.M.

6. ____ The Bible story is the most important part of the hour.

7. ____ Every preschool lesson has just three activities: arrival time, together time and handwork.

CHAPTER 8

LEARNING CENTERS ARE TEACHING CENTERS

Learning centers are places where children explore and discover! Learning centers give boys and girls a good opportunity to learn through seeing, hearing, touching, smelling and tasting. Learning centers provide preschool pupils with the variety and activity their short attention spans and growing bodies demand. Learning centers are teaching centers.

Preschool children are best taught through the use of learning centers. Each learning center is a separate location for learning. It is a physical area set up for an activity that teaches, reinforces, reviews, pictures or applies an idea, concept or fact to the child.[1] Well-taught preschool lessons will use six or more learning centers each Sunday morning.

Learning centers can be elaborate or simple depending on the facilities and finances of the Sunday school. A learning center can be a table, window, rug, bulletin board, easel, play area, or simply a cardboard box. Preschoolers learn as they are involved in the learning activities set up in each center.

Learning centers are teaching centers. Although the children learn through play, they are not just having fun at these centers. They are learning, reviewing or applying the Bible truth of the day. There is often much repetition between the activities, but preschoolers enjoy and need the repetition. The major concern is that only ONE CONCEPT or idea is taught each Sunday.

LEARNING CENTER POSSIBILITIES

1. Tables
2. Bulletin Boards
3. Windows
4. Book Racks

5. Rugs
6. Electrical Outlets
7. Cardboard Boxes

LEARNING CENTERS ARE CONVERSA-TION CENTERS

One of the most important ways a teacher can lead a learning center activity is through her CONVERSATION. The teacher repeats key thoughts at each learning center through words, songs, stories and one-on-one conversation. The teacher asks questions in order to discover the child's level of understanding. This continual conversation is important. If it is neglected, the activity can quickly deteriorate to busy work. Here is an example of good CONVERSATION at the art center.

We are going to make grass! We can't make grass like God makes it can we? Yes, Betty, God makes grass grow, doesn't He? But we can only make it with our crayons. We will put our grass on the bulletin board and make it look like a hill. God must like green because He made grass green. Johnny, how does God help the grass grow?

LEARNING CENTERS IN SMALL CLASSES

There are many locations for learning centers even in the smallest classroom. The bulletin board, floor, table, rug and corner of the room can all serve as learning centers. All learning centers are set up before the pupils begin arriving for Sunday school. In small classrooms, the same area of the room might be used for more than one learning center. When more than one learning center must occur in the same area of the room (for example, at the table), set up the first learning center activity ahead of time, but put the materials for each additional activity to occur at the table in a separate box. Brightly colored boxes are pretty and children look forward to discovering what fun activity will come from each box. By clearing the previously used materials and opening a box containing the supplies for the next learning center, a lesson can progress smoothly and rapidly.

Here is an example of a learning center lesson that would be taught in a small classroom.

MARCH 3—JESUS TELLS OF GOD'S CARE

AIM: The pupil will realize God's love and thank God for his clothing.

1. Nature Center—Bouquet of flowers
2. Home Center—Make cookies in the shape of flowers
3. Art Center—Make birds
4. Story Circle—Jesus cares for children
5. Play activity—Pretend to grow
6. Art Center—Bible story handwork
7. Music Center—Cassette recording
8. Worship time—"Thank God for Clothing"
9. Refreshment time—Eat flower cookies

Have the bouquet of flowers on the table as the children arrive. Talk about the beautiful colors and shapes of the flowers
God made. Then have the children make their flower cookies
(cookie dough, rolling pins and cookie cutters are already on
the table). After the cookies are baking in the church kitchen
(or toaster oven brought in to the classroom) open the first
box in which you have the art materials for making the birds.
Move the children away from the table to a story circle and
then lead them in the play activity. Open the second box in
which you have the handwork and materials needed for the
Bible story handwork. Move the children to another section
of the room where you have the cassette recorder for the
music time. Have a box of clothing ready to take out items
for the children to take turns praying, "Thank You, Jesus, for
giving me -----."This can be on another side of the room.
Gather back at the table to enjoy the flower cookies for refreshment time. Notice how the table was used for a learning center a number of times as the children moved from one
activity to another.

LEARNING CENTERS IN PRESCHOOL DEPARTMENTS

In a preschool department where there are several workers,
each teacher is assigned the responsibility of a learning center. Several learning-center activities can be going on at the
same time. Let's study the lesson on JESUS TELLS OF GOD'S
CARE and see what happens in a departmental setting.

Learning centers #1, #2 and #3 take place simul-
taneously during the arrival time and first 15 or 20
minutes of Sunday school. One teacher is at the art
center for making birds, a second teacher is at the
nature center with a bouquet of flowers and the
third teacher is prepared to help children make
cookies in the home-living center. The preschool
department superintendent welcomes children as
they arrive and directs them to a learning center.
Children can move from one center to another as
their interest directs.

The story circle is a "Together time" with everyone gathering on the story rug for the Bible story.

Learning activity #5 is a group activity where each teacher takes a few children to a wall and has them

pretend to grow by bending their knees and pushing their back up and down against the wall.

Learning center #6 is a Bible-story handwork time with each teacher taking a small group of children to a table.

Learning center #7 is a "Together time" with everyone coming together to listen to a recording and short story.

Learning activity #8 has each teacher taking a small group of children to a separate area of the room for prayer time. The children thank God for the items of clothing they have been given. Each teacher is in a different section of the room.

The class ends with a refreshment time, thanking
God for the cookies the children made earlier in the
hour.

A learning center is a physical area in the classroom set up
before class to teach children a biblical concept. The same
concept is taught through each learning center activity. Notice how the same lesson and learning center approach can
be used in both small and large classrooms.

FACTS TO REMEMBER

LEARNING CENTERS ARE TEACHING CENTERS.

**A LEARNING CENTER IS A PHYSICAL AREA IN
THE CLASSROOM SET UP TO TEACH A BIBLICAL
CONCEPT.**

**GUIDED CONVERSATION PREVENTS BUSY
WORK.**

**LEARNING CENTERS ARE ALWAYS SET UP BE-
FORE PUPILS ARRIVE.**

QUIZ

1. Without teacher guided CONVERSATION, learning centers

   can deteriorate to _____.

2. Well-taught preschool lessons utilize a minimum of __

   _____ learning centers each Sunday.

3. Seven learning activities are planned to teach _____

   _____ truth(s).

4. How does a teacher set up learning centers ahead of time
   when a table must be used for more than one learning
   center?

   _____

5. All learning centers are to be set up before _____.

6. How does the order in which learning center activities occur differ between a small class and a multiple-staff preschool department?

   _____

   _____

7. List six areas in a small classroom that can be used for
   learning centers.

   a. _____ d. _____

   b. _____ e. _____

   c. _____ f. _____

CHAPTER 9
ORGANIZING LEARNING CENTERS

Anything that pupils do can be set up in a section of your classroom and be called a learning center. Special equipment is not always needed. Remember a LEARNING CENTER is A PHYSICAL AREA IN THE CLASSROOM SET UP TO TEACH, REINFORCE, REVIEW, PICTURE OR APPLY AN IDEA, CONCEPT OR FACT TO THE CHILD. Many of the activities planned for a Sunday school hour can happen within a learning center if a physical area is set up for the activity. Many learning centers are temporary centers set up and taken down each week.

Nine permanent learning centers are described in this chapter. These centers can be used for unstructured free time or led by a teacher to reinforce the theme of the day. If your classroom is not equipped for these centers, you might plan to systematically add one new center to your room every three months.

Make your preschool classroom a learning center experience for your preschoolers—filled with activity and movement, but centered in Christ and His teachings. Learning centers require extra thought and planning, but the response of the children makes them well worth the effort.

BLOCK CENTER

Blocks are important learning tools as the young child works alone, in parallel play with another child or in cooperation with others. It provides many opportunities for sharing and helping. Block building can play an important role in developing a child's self-concept. At the block center the teacher can often initiate building projects to help the children become familiar with life in Bible times. Temples, walls, houses, churches, etc., are easy to build and frequently found in Bible stories.

Large blocks, usually 12 inches long and made of cardboard, commonly known as "Blockbusters" can be ordered from Christian Publications, Inc., 3825 Hartzdale Drive, Camp Hill, PA 17011. Blockbusters are recommended for toddlers and for two-year-olds or as a beginning set for any preschool department. Wooden unit blocks are expensive but ideal for three- to five-year-olds. They can be ordered from school supply firms.

HOME LIVING CENTER

The center of a preschool child's world is his house. Some children spend 24 hours a day, five to six days a week, in their home. For this reason the home living center is a vital part of the preschool department. It provides natural opportunities for him to play out familiar, everyday experiences. The home living area is a good place for the young child to practice the things he learns in Sunday school, such as taking turns, being kind, helping and obeying.

Basic home center equipment should include a cradle or doll bed and dolls. The children love them and they relate meaningfully to many Bible stories. Add a small table and chairs, cupboard or shelves for dishes and dress-up clothes. When possible add a sink and stove. The center can be used for unstructured play or teacher-led when it is part of the lesson plan.

NATURE CENTER

Exploring the things God has created helps the young child sense God's care and love. Provide a nature center with a large magnifying glass on a small table, shelf or windowsill. This center is the perfect opportunity to introduce materials for sensory experiences. Plants, flowers, growing seeds, autumn leaves, a bird's nest, shells, small animals and many seasonal items are fun for children to explore and discover. The nature center can be in the room at all times, even though it is not used every Sunday. Teachers add new items and direct children to it when lessons include nature center discoveries.

BOOK CENTER

Books are important learning tools for preschool children. A quiet corner with a slanted shelf book rack makes an ideal book center. Children enjoy looking at books alone, but better still to have someone read to them. If you are short of staff, invite an adult class member to come to Sunday school early, in time to read to children through the early part of Sunday school. The book center can also be a teacher-led activity, used to reinforce the aim for the day. Each child can be given a book and asked to look for theme pictures (for example, pictures of helping, food, children of other countries, animals or birds).

PUZZLE CENTER

When a child uses a puzzle he learns to think, reason and solve problems. Completing a puzzle gives a child a feeling of success and accomplishment and builds self-esteem. A teacher can observe emotional, mental and physical development as a child works on a puzzle. It provides quality one-on-one time with the child. Invest in good wooden puzzles. Keep them on a puzzle rack. Children can learn to help themselves to the puzzles and put them back when they are finished.

ART CENTER

Art center activities are important expressional activities which you will use almost every Sunday. The projects can be correlated with the theme of the day. Other art projects can be used for the joy of the activity. Art gives the child an opportunity to express what he thinks and feels.

Keep large crayons in small containers covered with pretty contact paper. Provide felt pens, child's scissors and paste. Include tempera paint, watercolors and play dough. Smocks made from old shirts should be provided for painting activities. Play dough has innumerable uses as lesson reinforcement. Include it often for unstructured play, such as between Sunday school and church time.

MUSIC CENTER

A music center is a teacher-led part of the hour. However, a song such as "Oh, Who Can Make a Flower?" can be sung at any time during the Sunday school hour. A record player, cassette recorder, auto harp and rhythm-band instruments can be a part of the music center. Music is so important that chapter 10 has been devoted to it.

BULLETIN BOARD CENTER

Many lesson materials will provide the teachers with pictures to use on the bulletin board. Each preschool department should build their own picture file. Children can enjoy and comment on these pictures. Occasionally the children can decorate a bulletin board as an expressional activity. If you don't have enough bulletin board space, fasten a piece of shelf paper on the wall. Children can draw pictures to illustrate a Bible truth or paste pictures (for example, leaves, snowflakes, animals, cars and people going to church) to shelf paper for the bulletin board. The ideal size for a preschool bulletin board is 3' × 8'. Attach the bottom of your board to the wall twelve inches above the floor.

CONVERSATION CENTER

Throughout your curriculum materials you will find an occasional conversation center. The plan is usually to show pictures or objects to direct the thinking of the children to the theme of the day. However, conversation is an art every teacher should develop and use at each learning center activity. *Guided conversation* is an important tool, but often overlooked. In order to use it effectively you will need to have a close relationship to the Lord and to the child. You will need to know about the family situation. (Be careful about "daddy" if there is no father in the home.) Plan for some key conversational thoughts to use at the center to which you are assigned. Use questions and brief comments to link the learning activity to the lesson aim. If your story is on the Good Samaritan, you will want to have in mind ways to direct the conversation to kindness. Recall Bible verses such as "Be . . . kind one to another." Even when putting away materials teach through your conversation: "This is the way we keep God's house neat and tidy. Helping in God's house is fun to do!"

QUIZ

1. A learning center is a _____

   .area set up for an activity that _____.

2. The center of a preschool child's world is his _____.

3. The nature center needs a large _____.

4. What is the ideal size for a preschool bulletin board?

   _____

5. Why are puzzles used in Sunday school?

   a. _____

   b. _____

6. List eight art supplies which should be included in an art center.

   a. _____   e. _____

   b. _____   f. _____

   c. _____   g. _____

   d. _____   h. _____

FACTS TO REMEMBER

LEARNING CENTERS ARE PLACES WHERE CHILDREN EXPLORE AND DISCOVER.

LEARNING CENTERS CAN BE TEMPORARY CENTERS.

CHAPTER 10
MUSIC WITH YOUNG CHILDREN

Music is one of the most valuable tools to help young children learn Bible truths. The words should be meaningful to the child and never symbolic. The songs in your curriculum materials are carefully written and selected to accompany the truths being taught. It is vitally important that you learn the recommended songs which are a basic part of the total-hour teaching plan.

TEACH THE MEANING OF MUSIC

The song becomes meaningful by the way it is taught! Before suggesting that the children sing the song, let them hear its message in various ways:

- Incorporate the song or its message into your conversation at any time throughout the hour.

- Use the song in nonstructured, casual ways at the learning centers.

- Incorporate the words of the song in the telling of the story.

- Use the song on a cassette (or record) to play softly during arrival time or during art activities.

- Always talk about the song. Introduce even familiar songs with a meaningful remark, "Let's sing about how we can all be good helpers in Sunday school," instead of, "Let's sing 'Helping.'"

- Illustrate the words of the song with large, colorful pictures.

USE MUSIC THROUGHOUT THE HOUR

In your curriculum there will be several songs suggested for each unit. The meaning of these songs is taught many times throughout the hour. The singing can be done at the art center, during the together times, in the middle of the Bible story, at the nature center or while working in the activity books. This repetition is a pleasant way for preschoolers to learn and remember the most important Bible truths. Attitudes are built through the frequent use of these songs. If you rely on old familiar choruses and fail to learn and teach the songs correlated with your lesson you are missing an important aspect of teaching preschoolers.

USE SPECIAL PURPOSE SONGS

Preschool children enjoy the teacher's singing. The Sunday school hour is made happy and pleasant when the teacher uses special purpose songs each week. Learn a song to help a shy child feel comfortable, "Do You Know This Friend of Mine?" Call the children together with "Oh Who Will Come and Sit with Me?" Learn welcome, prayer, Bible and thankyou songs and use them generously in teaching young children. Use a familiar tune such as "Here We Go 'Round the Mulberry Bush" or "The Farmer in the Dell" and make up words for any activity or idea you wish to teach. Don't be hesitant about singing. The quality of your voice does not matter. The joy in your song is what counts.

IMPORTANT POINTS TO REMEMBER

1. Avoid symbolism. "This Little Light," "A Sunbeam," "Deep and Wide" "Stand Alone on the Word of God" are examples of words to avoid. Use concrete words that are easily understood.

2. Avoid combining your group with older children for an opening exercise. The correlation of songs with the lesson

themes is far more important than learning songs which they don't understand. Remember that a piano and large group singing are not as important as singing with understanding.

3. Avoid a song service where you sing one song after another: "Now let's sing . . . now let's sing." Incorporate music at several points in the teaching hour.

4. Avoid forcing a child to participate. Remember that if a child simply listens, it is a learning experience. Gradually the child will sing occasional words and join the group.

INSTRUMENTS

Your VOICE is the most important piece of musical equipment your class will have. Don't be afraid to use your voice even if you aren't "choir material." A happy voice is much more desirable than one that can stay on tune. A piano is not necessary and is often a hindrance to spontaneous singing. However, a record player and cassette player are extremely important for the preschool classroom. Cassettes are sold with your curriculum and are of great assistance in teaching and learning new songs.

RHYTHM-BAND INSTRUMENTS should be a part of every preschool classroom. The enjoyment of the activity is more important than keeping time. Preschoolers may not be able to sing and play at the same time. Homemade rhythm band instruments are adequate. Consider making the following instruments:

> *Tambourines:* Aluminum pie plates to which Christmas bells are attached.
> *Drums:* Coffee cans with plastic lids. Cover with contact paper.
> *Shakers:* Beans or rice in small containers.
> *Rhythm sticks:* Quarter-inch dowels in 12-inch lengths.
> *Sandpaper Blocks:* Blocks of wood with coarse sandpaper firmly glued to each side.

QUIZ

1. Where does the teacher look to find excellent preschool songs that match the lesson theme? _____

2. A song becomes meaningful to preschoolers by the way it is _____.

3. What is built through the frequent use of music?_____

   _____

4. What is the most important piece of musical equipment in a preschool classroom? _____

5. The _____ of singing and music is more important than keeping time or being on tune.

6. List four types of special purpose songs that can be used to introduce class activities.

   a. _____ c. _____

   b. _____ d. _____

FACTS TO REMEMBER

SING IT OVER AND OVER AND OVER AND OVER.

USE MUSIC THROUGHOUT THE HOUR.

JOY IS MORE IMPORTANT THAN VOICE.

AVOID SYMBOLISM IN CHOOSING SONGS FOR YOUNG CHILDREN.

CHAPTER 11
LESSON PREPARATION

The quality of your teaching performance is greatly influenced by the time you spend in preparing a lesson. Two hours of preparation time is the minimum expectation of teachers. No two teachers prepare the same way because of differing work schedules and personalities. However, let's review *seven* principles every preschool teacher needs to follow in preparing a lesson.

PREPARE EARLY

Every teacher should have the lesson fully prepared by Friday night. When lessons are prepared on Saturday, it is often too late to utilize many of the good ideas the Holy Spirit will give you for the lesson. You may not have time to make visuals, gather pictures, purchase supplies and properly set up learning centers. When everything is in readiness, the session proceeds smoothly.

As you prepare, pray for each child individually.

WRITE THE AIM

Every lesson has one purpose, one aim. Every part of the Sunday school hour is designed to teach just one truth. Write out exactly what you want to accomplish through the session. EXAMPLE: Children will learn to be God's helper at home by putting the silverware on the table.

In a preschool classroom it helps to print the AIM on an 8″x12″ piece of construction paper and post it somewhere in the room where all staff members will be continually reminded of the theme of the day for conversation and activities.

LIVE THE LESSON

Read through the lesson early in the week. Find the central truth and ask God to show you how it applies to your life. Choose a personal application and do what God has led you to do. Since the stories are so familiar, preschool teachers sometimes miss this personal life application.

READ THE WHOLE LESSON

Unfortunately many teachers do not follow the teaching plan as outlined in their teacher's manual. Visuals are not used, songs are not learned, creative methods are replaced with teacher talks and learning center suggestions ignored. Curriculum publishers try to be creative and build variety into their lesson plans, but teachers tend to force the lesson into a familiar pattern week after week. As you read the material, circle every suggested teaching activity and the enrichment ideas. Utilize the professional advice the teacher's manual offers.

PREPARE A LESSON PLAN

Use the "LESSON PLANNING SHEET" on page 30 to prepare your lesson plan. If you are the department superintendent, you will prepare the "Lesson Planning Sheet" and distribute it to the staff at least a week before it is needed. It is important for all members of the teaching team to be familiar with all of the material in the teacher's manual. Knowledgeable teachers can work together as A TEAM.

PREPARE THE STORY

Teachers may take turns telling the story. Never read the Bible story. If needed, make notes to have in your Bible as a guide. Prepare thoroughly so you can leave the manual at home. The Bible story is central to the entire hour. Learn to tell it well!

Tell the story within the child's interest and experience. Tell the story with the Bible open so pupils will know its source. Speak clearly and slowly with change of pace and tone of voice. Speak quietly to children whenever possible. A quiet voice is more of an attention-getter than a loud, demanding voice. Be enthusiastic, be dramatic. Use lots of action words—dialogue and imagination! Be sure to remember the child's short attention span. Very short stories for two-year-olds.

You have heard the saying, "Practice makes perfect." Verbally practicing the story before class will significantly improve your story telling abilities. Consider each story as if it were going to be shown on public television with thousands of people listening. Your stories are more than performance, but the easier you make it for pupils to listen, the more they will remember. After your story is prepared, go to your bedroom, shut the door and verbally practice in front of a mirror. Practice being dramatic, emphasizing key phrases.

PREPARE YOUR ROOM

Preparing the room is usually the responsibility of the department superintendent, but it can be shared with other staff members. Sometime during the week or early on Sunday morning prepare your classroom. Make sure that the room is clean and tidy. Update your bulletin boards. Lay out the materials you need at the learning centers. Organize the visuals you will need for the story. When everything is in readiness, you can give your undivided attention to the first arrival.

FACTS TO REMEMBER

USE THE PROFESSIONAL ADVICE FOUND IN THE TEACHER'S MANUAL.

TEACHING PERFORMANCE IS GREATLY INFLUENCED BY PREPARATION TIME.

WHEN EVERYTHING IS IN READINESS, THE SESSION WILL RUN SMOOTHLY.

EVERY LESSON HAS ONE PURPOSE, ONE AIM.

QUIZ

MULTIPLE-CHOICE QUESTIONS: (CIRCLE THE BEST ANSWER)

1. When a Sunday school lesson is prepared at the last minute:

   a) Not enough prayer has preceded preparation.
   b) The Holy Spirit cannot work.
   c) The teacher cannot implement many good teaching ideas.

2. Understanding the central truth early in the week allows the teacher to:

   a) Thoroughly prepare the lesson.
   b) Apply the lesson to one's own life.
   c) Gather materials and prepare visuals.
   d) Do all of the above.

COMPLETION QUESTIONS

3. The Sunday school lesson should be fully prepared by

   _____

4. The teacher should _____ the Bible story before telling it to the children.

5. Preparing the preschool room is important so the teachers can give their undivided _____ to the first arrivals.

6. What is the minimum preparation time for a preschool teacher who must write out the lesson plan?_____

7. Why is it helpful to post the aim in a multiple-staff preschool classroom?

CHAPTER 12
PARENT TEACHER RELATIONSHIPS

Our program with preschool children will be incomplete unless it can be reinforced in the home. Cooperation and support between the Sunday school and the home can provide positive reinforcement.

How can you as a concerned teacher provide this reinforcement and encouragement? How can you help young Christian families build a strong family unit? What can you do for children who come from a nonchurch background? How can you reach and help the single parent?

For each of these situations, it is important for the teacher to spend time with parents. All parents will respond to love and friendship. All teachers need the insights and support the parents can give.

SUNDAY MORNING

To make the best use of the brief contacts on Sunday morning, it is essential that everything be in readiness in the room well before the hour to begin. If the staff is present 15 minutes before the starting hour with learning center activities ready for the earliest arrival, then one of the staff members can be at the door ready with a warm and friendly greeting. The same is true for a well-planned transitional period between Sunday school and church.

INVITE PARENTS TO VISIT THE DE-PARTMENT

At some time during the year, schedule all parents to have a turn at spending a morning in the classroom. Parents will become familiar with your procedures and expectations. They can join in the songs and see the value of the pupil take-home materials and activity books. Provide chairs away from the centers of activity. Don't be too concerned if their presence affects the child. Plan to reserve time after Sunday school to answer any questions.

CONTACTS WITH THE HOME

1. **Use the Mail.** A quarterly letter to the home can be of great benefit in highlighting your program and objectives. In addition to this formal type of communication, use handwritten notes and cards with expressions of friendship. Young children are excited about getting mail too!

2. **Use the Phone.** Frequent friendly calls can help to build bridges. These calls should not be limited to absentee follow-up.

3. **Plan Parents' Meetings.** Invite the mothers of your children to your home for informal get-acquainted times. Limit these meetings to three or four parents. If at all possible plan quarterly meetings with parents to discuss goals. Share with the parents pictures you have taken of the children's activities. Provide a small bulletin board near the door of your room to post pictures.

4. **Make Home Visits.** There is nothing more effective in building relationships with parents than to visit them and their preschooler at home. Look for special reasons to call in the home. Bring a small birthday gift. If there has been an absence, bring the take-home materials. The key here is to give something rather than to convey the attitude "where were you?" Keep records of all home visits so no child is overlooked.

Home visits are encouraged by assigning each preschool teacher four or five children. The teachers are responsible for follow-up, parental relationships and home visits pertaining to their children.

INVOLVE THE PARENTS

Parents will be more interested if they are asked to assist in various ways. Some mothers will be glad to prepare refreshments and to assist with a party. Others may be willing to assist with the preparation of handwork. Be on the lookout for fathers with carpentry experience if you need to have cupboards or a doll bed built. Occasionally you may wish to use a parent to assist at one of the learning centers when a teacher is absent. Look for ways to make parents feel needed and appreciated.

Always remember that your attitude needs to be one of working with parents, not for parents. Such an attitude is reflected in this note:

> Dear Karen:
>
> I am enclosing an outline of some of the things we are trying to accomplish in our Sunday school class. No doubt you are working on some of these same things with Johnny at home. Would you be willing to check the things that should be emphasized with Johnny and add others which you feel need consideration?
>
> Thank you

The preschool program is incomplete unless it is reinforced in the home. Build relationships with parents and you will build positive home reinforcement.

QUIZ

1. A preschool Sunday school program is incomplete without the reinforcement of the _____.

2. In building relationships with parents, nothing is more effective than _____.

3. In visiting the home of an absent preschooler it is important to _____.

4. Teachers need to develop an attitude of 'working _____ parents, rather than _____ parents.

5. List four ways a preschool teacher can involve parents in the preschool program.

   a. _____

   b. _____

   c. _____

   d. _____

FACTS TO REMEMBER

WORK WITH PARENTS, NOT FOR PARENTS.

ALWAYS GIVE THE PARENTS SOMETHING WHEN VISITING THE YOUNG CHILD'S HOME.

TEACHER WITH PARENT IS A COMPLETE TEAM.

CHAPTER 13
LOVE MAKES THE DIFFERENCE

Julie was just entering the beginner class. It wasn't a significant event. Julie, our daughter, was just changing classes.

Four weeks later, the phone rang and a pleasant voice asked to speak with Julie. This was a bit unusual because four-year-olds don't get a lot of phone calls. Julie came to the phone, listened a couple of minutes, put the phone down and came to me asking,

"Daddy, can I help my teacher make cookies? She needs my help!"

Sure enough, this teacher had called asking if she could pick up Julie so they could make cookies together. We were delighted to say, "Yes."

A month or two passed when Julie received another phone call. This time Mrs. Fetter, Julie's teacher, needed help pushing her shopping cart at the grocery store. The grocery cart experience was quite exciting to Julie. I am sure the store manager became a little excited also seeing our four-year-old pushing a cart around his nicely displayed merchandise.

Later Julie was asked to help Mrs. Fetter baby-sit. Julie's teacher was a foster parent for babies and at times had two or three infants. Fully confident in her baby-sitting abilities, Julie went off to baby-sit with Mrs. Fetter.

One Sunday, as I came up from the church basement into the church foyer, my eye caught sight of a Yogi Bear button. It was hard to miss these buttons because they were about four inches across and pinned to the chest of every four- and five-year-old child. A four-inch button on a small child looks like a twelve-inch button. We soon located Julie and she proudly displayed her Yogi Bear button. Upon closer examination, we noted that each button was handmade, colored with felt-tip markers, laminated with clear contact paper and mounted on firm cardboard. It could have easily taken someone more than twenty minutes to make just one of these buttons.

Julie spent two delightful years with Mrs. Fetter. I learned through studying the roll books that Mrs. Fetter's class of four- and five-year-olds had grown from an average attendance of eight to more than twenty-five in two years. Did this growth come because Mrs. Fetter was a skilled teacher? Maybe. I never saw her teach. I do know that Mrs. Fetter loved Julie and our daughter loved her. Love made the difference to Julie and apparently to twenty-four other children and their parents.

The apostle John points to God the Father as the supreme example of love. In First John 4:9–10 he lists three qualities of love:

"This is love: not that we loved God, but that he loved us and sent his Son as the atoning sacrifice for our sins."

Notice how God first loved us. **LOVE TAKES THE INITIATIVE.** Often we wait for others to reach out to us before we respond positively toward them. The preschool child cannot reach out to you. You must continually take the initiative in showing love and concern for your pupils. Mrs. Fetter showed this initiative in phoning Julie, making buttons and repeatedly doing nice things for her pupils.

LOVE ACTS SACRIFICIALLY. Notice how God first loved us, but His love was backed by ACTION. Love is more than a feeling or attitude. Love is action. It was a sacrificial action for God to send His only Son. When the teacher loves her pupils, she gives away part of herself. Our losses may be measured in time, energy, money and inconvenience. The sacrifices of love may not always hurt, but they always demand that we give up something. Mrs. Fetter gave up a lot of time making Yogi Bear buttons. It was not convenient for her to take a four-year-old grocery shopping. She could have made those cookies much faster without a little helper. But she loved and love acts sacrificially.

God's loving action was directed at meeting a real need, our sin. **LOVE ACTS SACRIFICIALLY TO MEET NEEDS.** Your pupils have needs. They need to know about God, Jesus and the Word of God. They need a loving teacher who makes Sunday school a joy. They get sick and need get-well cards or the loving visit of a teacher with a box of popsicles. The preschool teacher is preparing the young child so that at the proper time through the enabling of the Holy Spirit, he will express faith in Christ and become a born-again child of God's family. A young child needs to be prepared so the Word of God can take root and grow up in his life.

Love is taking the initiative and acting sacrificially to meet the needs of others. As you enter the classroom in the weeks to come, take the initiative and show love outside the classroom. Give up some of your time, energy, convenience and money for the sake of your students. Meet the needs of your young children.

> *If I teach in the tongues of men and of angels, but have not love, I am only a resounding gong or a clanging cymbal. If I have the gift of prophecy and can fathom all mysteries and all knowledge, and if I have a faith that can move mountains, but have not love, I am nothing. If I give all I possess to (my Sunday school) and surrender my body to the flames, but have not love, I gain nothing* (I Corinthians 13:1–3 NIV).

—Daryl Dale

TEACHING BASICS: PRESCHOOL BIBLIOGRAPHY

NOTES

Chapter 8

1. Rachel Lee, *Learning Centers for Better Christian Education,* p. 29.

BIBLIOGRAPHY

Barbour, Mary A. *You Can Teach 2s and 3s.* Wheaton: Victor Books, 1981.

Harrel, Donna and Wesley Haystead. *Creative Bible Learning for Young Children, Birth–5 Years.* Glendale: Regal Books, 1977.

Hutton, Delores. *Sunday School Activities for Preschool Children.* Grand Rapids: Baker Book House, 1979.

Klein, Karen. *How to Do Bible Learning Activities, Ages 2–5.* Ventura, CA: Gospel Light Publications, 1982.

LeBar, Mary and Betty Riley. *You Can Teach 4s and 5s.* Wheaton: Victor Books, 1981.

Lee, Rachel. *Learning Centers for Better Christian Education.* Valley Forge, PA: Judson Press, 1982.

—————— *Make Your Own Preschool Furniture (Patterns).* Nashville: Convention Press, 1979.

Neuen, Thelma F. *Toddler Teacher's Guide.* Wheaton: Scripture Press, 1977.

Strickland, Jenell. *How to Guide Preschoolers.* Nashville: Convention Press, 1982.